CABBAGES & ROSES

AT HOME
WITH COUNTRY

CABBAGES & ROSES

At HOME
with COUNTRY

BRINGING THE COMFORTS OF COUNTRY HOME

CHRISTINA STRUTT

with *Amy Gibbons and* Kate Strutt
Photography by Edina van der Wyck

CICO BOOKS
LONDON NEW YORK

Text: Kate Strutt

Editor: Zia Mattocks

Designer: Paul Tilby

Photographer: Edina van der Wyck

Published in 2010 by CICO Books
An imprint of Ryland Peters & Small Ltd
20–21 Jockey's Fields   519 Broadway, 5th Floor
London WC1R 4BW   New York NY 10012

www.cicobooks.com

10 9 8 7 6 5 4 3 2 1

A CIP catalog record for this book is available from
the Library of Congress and the British Library.

ISBN 978 1 907030 16 1

Printed in China

CONTENTS

FOREWORD BY TRICIA FOLEY

The name Cabbages & Roses has always conjured up fond memories of Mr McGregor's garden, bouquets of fragrant old roses, and the classic English style that is so familiar and loved by me.

Growing up in America with my English grandmother, the cupboards were always filled with pretty teacups and the sofas were cozy with floral chintz cushions. I learned from her a pride in homekeeping, a love of all things "English": taking pleasure in flower gardens and always making time for a cup of tea and a chat.

When Christina asked to include my home in her book, I was so pleased and looked forward to seeing all the natural linens and soft florals that she is known for nestled in among my simple furnishings. I knew that they would be just right and "at home in the country" here. The natural materials and soft colors of the Cabbages & Roses' furnishings celebrate and interpret classic English country design for today and bring comfort and joy to all our homes.

Tricia Foley

Long Island, November 2009

INTRODUCTION

In these troubled times, there are few things that raise the spirit more than creating a welcoming home filled with the treasures that make life rich and fulfilling. The near fatal collapse of our banking systems, the credit crunch, and the perilous situation in the job market have brought us all down to earth with a bump. I, for one, think this is the best thing that could have happened to our greedy culture of living way beyond our means and our lack of respect for the things we so take for granted. Statistically, home has become of greater consequence and family is now more important than ever—just as it should be.

Cabbages & Roses has stood its ground for the ten years it has been alive. We have gently grown and expanded, whispering rather than shouting, quietly infiltrating lives and homes throughout the world in the nicest possible way. We have grown up and our range has grown up with us. In this beautiful new book we have visited homes in England and in America, seeing where our products have found themselves in completely diverse situations from tents in the English countryside to New York loft apartments—it is this ability to fit in anywhere, enhancing rather than detracting, that makes Cabbages & Roses the success it is today.

So, here it is—our fifth book, our new collections, our style, our vision in print.

Christina Strutt

BROOK COTTAGE

IN THE SIXTEENTH CENTURY, BROOK COTTAGE WAS A WATER MILL ON A GREGORIAN MONASTIC ESTATE, WITH A STREAM RUNNING BETWEEN TWO RUDIMENTARY COTTAGES THAT HAVE BEEN GRADUALLY LINKED TOGETHER OVER THE YEARS. STEEPED IN HISTORY AND NATURAL GRANDEUR, THIS WAS THE PLACE IN WHICH I IMMEDIATELY KNEW I WOULD FLOURISH, THE HOME WHERE I COULD ESTABLISH MYSELF AND MY FAMILY, AND EVENTUALLY MY COMPANY CABBAGES & ROSES.

Medieval structures are a joy to work with because they are bossy—you can't change what is already there. The small windows are not very generous with light, but the nooks and crannies make up for it tenfold. With all houses there are compromises you have to make, and the best approach is to be optimistic and try to visualize ways to take advantage of any quirks rather than hiding them.

LEFT The tones used in the kitchen are not necessarily "traditional" country, but they are all in sync with one another. The wicker baskets, cream ceramics, glass, and zinc are perfectly in tune with the walls and woodwork in a mixture of modern heritage-style colors and old pigmented paint layered up over the years to give depth. The mood is altered by the changing light outside, reflected by the wide windowsill.

ABOVE LEFT An old black-and-white saucer used as a makeshift butter dish blends into the stronger slate gray of the tablecloth. The shock of daffodil yellow disarms the solid color of the printed linen and brings a ray of spring sunshine into the room.

ABOVE RIGHT A collection of old and new jugs and pitchers add to the layers of different shades of white and cream dotted around the kitchen, with a display of old postcards in correlating tones bringing back fond memories.

It has long been asserted that the kitchen is the heart of a home, and we are fortunate enough to have a house where this is true in all senses. The kitchen is in the center of the house, complete with a fireplace and a staircase winding up to the bedrooms. It is where the majority of visitors are entertained, and the layout has been designed to provide all the crucial elements for creating a perfect space for comfortable socializing and cooking.

I love the apparent mishmash of color and texture that pulls together to make a coherent scheme—the recurring creams and silvers, grays, and blacks give this traditional kitchen a slight edge which prevents it from feeling too quaint. The result is a stimulating space with plenty to feed the eye and mind.

A ROARING FIRE AND A WELCOMING SOFA IN THE KITCHEN ARE THE ULTIMATE COUNTRY LUXURY.

OPPOSITE The monotone dresser, though traditional in style, looks clean and contemporary with the repetitions of similar objects and colors. I keep an eye out for anything in tune with the fresh tones of white and sparkling glass. Almost everything in the kitchen has been chosen either for its beauty or its functionality, creating a working display of kitchen utensils that are both practical and pleasing to the eye. The natural rhythm of use keeps the dust at bay and the display fluid.

LEFT, TOP Random objects are collected over a lifetime. The best ones survive reshuffles and decluttering over the years, and each piece has a natural rhythm and place in the house, the summer season bringing a fresh green sprig to rest next to a beautiful apple-green book handed down through generations of readers.

OPPOSITE, BOTTOM, AND THIS PAGE The eclectic display on the reclaimed wooden fire surround brings a sense of informality to the parlor. Old toys and childhood memories bide their time. Chipped vintage dishes provide useful storage for candles, spare buttons, and other trinkets. Cake stands piled high with dried fruit and a moss wreath retrieved from the box of Christmas decorations for a spring outing give height to the collection of treasures. The large twig wreath adds drama and provides a central focus.

OPPOSITE The battered, white-painted chair and print cushion lift and lighten this corner of the parlor, while the crumpled linen tablecloth counters the more formal striped curtains. The hand-sewn rabbit perching on the shelf—within speaking distance of the cricketers—was made for me by the Cabbages & Roses girls in the London shop and has been treasured ever since.

RIGHT My cherished collections of vintage books are ever-increasing, being bought for their covers or sweet titles as much as for their contents. Books are an invaluable source of decoration, warmth, and character in any house. A notebook printed with a 1950s photograph of my sister Anne on the cover adds to the mishmash of boxes, books, pencil pots, and paints housed on the built-in shelves.

The fabrics used in the kitchen are constantly changing, to reflect the mood I am in, the flowers that are in season and blooming in the garden, or whatever clean linen I find in the cupboard. The thing that holds it all together as a scheme, in keeping with the tone of the house, is the sense of history, of the people who live there and the things they have collected to create their home.

The parlor used to be the kitchen, but is now a multipurpose room with a large table for me to work on, which can also be used for dining when it is too cold to eat outside or there are too many people to seat in the kitchen. It is full to the brim with books, trinkets, and pictures to feed my creativity when I am designing new collections. The array of colors in the book spines and pictures work well with the reds in the fabrics, giving a comfortable, welcoming feel. The key to creating a space where tasks are to be performed is to fill it with personal items that inspire you and put you at ease.

I am a firm believer that any style of interior design should let a house be lived in. My sitting room accommodates family, visitors, and pets, with all their ensuing clutter, and allows them to relax and be comfortable. Plenty of tables and shelves for display and storage give order to antiques, books, and eclectic treasures, ensuring that they don't become overwhelming. The pale tones of the vintage quilt on the sofa lighten the effect of the deep reds used in the room. The quilt can be washed frequently, making it a practical as well as a beautiful addition to the room.

Creating a display of pictures—even one that is slightly chaotic and diverse in style—is a great way to add a point of interest to a room. The pictures that someone collects over time reveal a huge amount about them. It takes confidence to hang the pictures you have chosen for all to view. Through the years I have been drawn to some unusual and wide-ranging picture subjects, and as my collection has grown, I have learned how to create very different atmospheres in various rooms by hanging the pictures I feel sit well together. Here in the parlor, I have tried to play to the warmth of the wood of the rustic antique side table and bottle carrier, which acts as a gentle foil to the mishmash of pictures of the wall behind.

As the parlor is used for many different tasks and occasions, the furniture often needs to be reshuffled in order to accommodate a meeting or a dinner party. The lighting in the room is key to its success as a study and a dining room, both having very different lighting requirements, so I have accumulated various lamps, lamp shades, and lanterns to brighten up the room as required. For nighttime dining, the room is lit only by candles, which cast a flattering light with dramatic shadows, and create an intimate atmosphere. As in the kitchen, the china on display in the parlor is also used for serving food, so there is a natural turnaround of decorative and functional objects.

A NEUTRAL BACKDROP OF PLAIN WALLS AND FLOORS GIVES BUSY DISPLAYS OF PICTURES OR ECLECTIC COLLECTIONS OF OBJECTS AND ANTIQUES THE OPPORTUNITY TO BREATHE.

The neutral walls and limestone floor essentially "cleanse the palette," forming a simple backdrop to the chaos of the pictures and letting the space as a whole exude a sense of calm. This makes it easy to dress up the room for special occasions and to change its nature at the drop of a hat. The variety and depth of colors and textures introduced by the fabrics, pictures, and other decorative objects—including a large rug in winter—ensures that the parlor never feels cold or too formal.

OPPOSITE A toy sailing boat adds some cheer to two very austere family portraits, affectionately named "The Aunts." Mirrors waiting for some wall space don't look out of place lying in an old butler's tray.

ABOVE The balance of light and dark, the generous use of pictures, and the minimal, useful clutter softened by the occasional print cushion result in a calm atmosphere that doesn't feel sterile or untouchable. The original dark beams were painted white to brighten the room and make the low ceiling seem higher.

Nothing is more satisfying than climbing up into a high bed—it feels luxurious, old-fashioned, cozy, and grand. Here, the height of the nightstands has been adjusted to keep everything in proportion, and the wall, which is cut short by the sloping ceiling, is made to look wider by the simple symmetry of the pictures. Color and pattern are introduced through the combination of fabrics in similar hues—from the curtains, to the box files, to the twin headboards that have been joined together and upholstered, to the vintage patchwork quilt.

Over the course of 30 years or so, the main bedroom has gradually evolved into my ultimate peaceful sanctuary. It has substantially increased in size, becoming one of the largest rooms in the house, after an internal wall was knocked down to enable the generously proportioned square room to unfold to its full potential.

To the right of the much-used fireplace is the entrance to the walk-in closet, a teardrop-shaped arch formed between two old chimneys, whose unusual shape gives the room a gothic twist. Three steps lead up into the space, which is used for hanging clothes but also has ample storage in the eaves for boxes of Christmas decorations.

A SCATTERING OF BLACK PICTURE FRAMES ADDS A MASCULINE TOUCH TO A FEMININE BEDROOM AND IS ALL THAT IS NEEDED TO GIVE THE ROOM A SENSE OF BALANCE.

The luxurious pale carpet was perhaps an unwise choice for someone with two cats, two dogs, and an apparent inability to remove muddy shoes—but the lightness and sense of comfort that it brings to the room are worth the anxiety of keeping it clean.

ABOVE A Gothic doorway and old fireplace imbue the bedroom with a slightly eccentric feel. All manner of trinkets are displayed on every surface, including a small toy chicken, once an Easter decoration, perched upside-down inside an old birdcage—the fact that it has never been successfully placed upright has become an affectionate joke over the years.

The floral curtains and delicate pale pink printed linen cloth that covers the long dressing table are offset by the black picture frames that are scattered over the walls. These echo the fireplace and grate, and together introduce a strong masculine element to the bedroom.

Every available surface in the bedroom is filled with decorative objects—no matter how many culls there have been, there always seems to be a surfeit. Family heirlooms, photographs, dishes, jars, and vases of flowers jostle for space with files, notebooks, and jewelry boxes.

The wooden towel rail and gilt frames of the Victorian landscapes add touches of warmth to the whites and blues, a color scheme that could otherwise seem cold and sterile. The white-framed mirrors bounce the light around and add apparent space.

In spite of the small windows in the bedroom and adjoining bathroom, the pale, reflective surfaces bounce the natural light around, making the interiors feel bright and airy, especially in the morning when the sun shines directly onto this side of the house. The simple bathroom is painted plain white, with tongue-and-groove paneling on the built-in bathtub and vanity unit, and understated furnishings including a wooden towel rail, rustic hooks for bathrobes and towels, and a battered painted table. Accents of soft blue are introduced through the woven rug, the towels, a laundry bag in a Cabbages & Roses print, and the Victorian plates on the wall. The fresh, cool tones are complemented by the utilitarian metal and glass containers, while gilt framed prints and an oversized mirror add interest and a hint of drama.

Every corner of Brook Cottage has evolved during the years my family has made it our home. Each room is brimming with memories, atmosphere, and personality, while somehow managing to be a living, working entity that is not restrained in any way. China can be chipped, cushions can be unplumped, carpets can be muddied, but the essence of this cozy home will always be present.

EVERY ROOM SHOULD REFLECT THE PERSONALITIES OF THE PEOPLE WHO LIVE IN THEM AND EXUDE A WELCOMING, RELAXING ATMOSPHERE WHILE REMAINING FUNCTIONAL AND PRACTICAL.

ABOVE A built-in vanity unit is a practical option when space is at a premium, providing ample storage for unsightly clutter. It lets this corner be calm as well as decorative, with a blue floral towel that is as ornamental as the Victorian plates on the wall.

OPPOSITE Seagrass carpet gives a modern twist to a long corridor, where a traditional armchair has been given a new look with a red check slipcover. The colors warm the cooler green and blue, and make the eclectic group of gothic pictures seem less formal.

BOTTOM LEFT A glimpse of a sunny haven hidden among the rambling gravel paths that navigate their way across the more formal part of the garden. The edge of the eleventh-century church reveals the historic importance of the site.

HANHAM COURT

THIS HISTORIC HOUSE IN SOMERSET HAS BEEN EVOLVING SINCE THE ELEVENTH CENTURY AND COMPRISES A NORMAN BARN, TUDOR GABLES, NINETEENTH-CENTURY EXTENSIONS, AND ARCHES JOINING UP THE VARIOUS PARTS. THE STRENGTHS AND BEAUTY OF THE HOUSE HAVE BEEN NURTURED AND THE BEST PARTS HAVE SURVIVED AND FLOURISHED. THE PROCESS OF ENRICHMENT HAS CONTINUED UNDER THE CURRENT OWNERS, WHO HAVE LIVED HERE FOR 15 YEARS. IT HAS BECOME A COLLABORATION OF DIFFERENT CENTURIES AND THE KNOWLEDGE THEY HAVE ACCUMULATED THROUGH YEARS OF TRAVELING, DISCOVERING AND CREATING RENOWNED GARDENS, RUINS, AND WATER SCULPTURES.

The owners have respected their role as guardians and caretakers of the house and the great chunk of British history that it has been witness to. Their efforts in custodianship have been so committed that they even planted an acorn taken from a historic oak tree that was felled by a storm outside the adjoining church. Their recognition that the house has survived kings, queens, wars, the dissolution of the monasteries, and man landing on the moon, has lead to a robust, intense,

ABOVE A corner of the medieval house in all its rustic glory. A display of antlers from past shooting parties doubles as perfect random hat stands—requiring a fishing net to recover the appropriate style.

and careful restoration of this family dwelling that has in no way detracted from the history that has created it. Austere monastic walls and constructions of winding wood clash with tongue-in-cheek collections and splashes of brilliant color, encircled outside by the magnificent gardens, created from scratch. It is a vast space to fill, but over the years of assembling the stuff of life and family, this strategic fortress overlooking the River Avon has evolved to become, above all, a family home—and recently a spectacle open to public view.

Throughout the house, color is used to full effect, with soothing greens, acid yellows, rich reds, deep velvety purples, and soft lavenders taking you on a meandering journey, just as they do in the garden. Collections of ancient paintings in black or gilt frames are hung against yolk-yellow walls above the well-worn flagstones and wide oak floorboards. The creaky staircase with imposing carved banisters plays host to a 1960s-style chair. A display of antlers and hats, fishing nets, and gardening tools looks just as at home against the grand oak paneling as a collection of priceless paintings or tapestries. Here, anything goes and everything works.

OPPOSITE Gilt frames, oversized portraits, and a coat of arms play to the immense grandeur and sheer impressiveness of the restored carved solid wood staircase.

RIGHT A hidden door leads from the central main hall to the small hexagonal music room with its high ceiling. Piles of sheet music offset the formality of a grand chandelier and mahogany piano.

ABOVE This old architectural miniature model of a Russian monastery outside Moscow is believed to have been a kind of nineteenth-century toy, and adds character to the room.

OPPOSITE The private sitting room houses a wonderful mix of pictures and treasured objects that collectively become a deeply personal retrospective of family life. The disused fireplace gives refuge to a Roman bust, which shares the space with an abandoned bird's nest of giant pine cones.

The house entertains trails of visitors, friends, and family, not to mention playing host to gardening courses and creative meetings where larger-than-life projects are born—most notably, designs for the Prince of Wales's garden at Highgrove House, Lord Andrew Lloyd Webber's estate at Sidmonton, and formal gardens for clients around the globe. For the amount of activity that prevails in the building, pieces such as a stone altar, used as a hall table, hold their own and give the house a feeling of solidity, as well as a witty and irreverent tone.

In the sanctuary of the library, deep red walls exude a cozy womb-like atmosphere, and acres of wall space adorned with well-read books create a studious feel. Hand-carved fire surrounds and bookcases built like

ABOVE LEFT AND RIGHT The library's crenelated bookcases emulate the random sections of fortressed roofing outside. The red pigment paint on the walls warms the vast room and provides a stimulating scholarly backdrop for creating and researching new projects. The gothic castellation theme is continued with turreted lamps and cabinets. Tall deep-set windows give views over the formal lawn to the wildflower meadows and meandering River Avon in the distance.

gothic towers are filled to overflowing with collections of occasionally kitsch, occasionally classic mementos.

The family accommodation sprawls through winding corridors and outbuildings, bringing life into each hidden space. A forgotten room has been turned into a gallery to display photos of home-grown flowers, while a gypsy caravan has found a home in a once unused courtyard.

Beyond the library door is the walkway leading between the kitchen stairs, entrance hall, and grand hall. The giant globe perching amid the gold embellishments on a sturdy marble table provides an eccentric and powerful welcome into the main entrance. The Gothic elements are in keeping with the period of this part of the house.

LEFT A private corner in the labyrinth of attic space serves as a library offshoot for the ever-increasing collection of old books. The hatted sculpture keeps a watchful eye over the collection.

OPPOSITE A light-filled spare bedroom is decorated with simple furniture that doesn't detract from the beauty of the old whitewashed walls. Pictures slot in anywhere the odd angles and sloping roof will allow, while faded linens keep the space looking fresh and clean.

THE ATTIC ROOMS HAVE
A DREAMY, ENCHANTING
QUALITY THAT MAKES THEM
A TRANQUIL HAVEN FROM
THE BUSTLE AND ENERGY
OF THE REST OF THE HOUSE.

Attic space and secret doors are some of the most extraordinary assets of ancient buildings. As you ramble along the attic corridors, with their uneven oak floors and old plastered walls, glancing out of slit windows onto the restored gargoyles, it is hard not to become disorientated. The views that sprawl from the top of the building disarm the senses, the formal lawns below take on a different aspect, and a wonky treehouse appears alarmingly close to toppling off the tree to which it has been attached.

A softer tenor is found up in the attic rooms, making cozy and secluded havens away from the bustle of life downstairs. Framed watercolor and oil paintings hang on the winding walls of the corridors off which the attic bedrooms are found, and more bookshelves line the remaining wall space. The raw plasterwork has been lovingly restored to its original state, unassuming and comfortable alongside the well-loved furniture that has followed the family from home to home.

In the guest bedrooms, where vintage quilts are stashed away in readiness for the chilly nights and deep frosts of an English winter, disproportionate furniture plays to the Alice in Wonderland character of the place. A tiny frail chair is dwarfed by the giant bed alongside it, while in another room a tall padded headboard squashes a painting up into the eaves. Tucked-away rooms and forgotten possessions let a guest feel a small sense of excitement when they rediscover a beautiful find from a flea market, or a treasure brought home from a Himalayan adventure by their hosts.

Portraits
David Wynne
May 17–June
Fitzwilliam M

As In the rest of the house, the smooth,
worn limestone of the windowsill and frame
speaks volumes of the centuries of wear
and tear it has endured. Along with the
raspberry floral curtains and vintage cotton
quilt, the crystal pendant lamp brings
femininity to the space, while the dark
wooden furniture results in a good balance.

ABOVE Strong black-framed etchings hold their own next to the dark wood and bright yellow walls. A slightly modern twist is welcome, with retro pieces like the battered old license plate and enamel pots.

RIGHT Large freestanding furniture is miniaturized by the generous scale of this bathroom. Having a bathroom large enough to play with the symmetry of retro chairs and huge bright artworks is truly a luxury.

The bathrooms take full advantage of the space available. A roll-top bathtub and large freestanding cupboard sit comfortably next to a vast wall hanging. Good ventilation in these huge rooms allows for them to be decorated and furnished as any other room might be, since prized paintings and antique furniture are not at risk of being damaged by steam or dampened by long, indulgent bathing.

The bathroom door blends in with the painted wood paneling to create a consistent border around the room. The untreated oak floorboards are protected with a simple bathmat, and frivolities such as curtains are rejected in favor of strong prints and urbane pictures to provide interesting focal points.

OPPOSITE The mix of old woods and vintage linens is complemented by industrial rusted lamps and retro school chairs, restored and painted in a cheerful cherry red and brightening the whitewashed room with brave splashes of color. The generous size of the French doors opening onto the veranda and garden make for a beautifully airy room.

RIGHT The walls of the studio in an outhouse are lined with white-painted paneling, a good foil for a collection of colorful items, coincidentally mimicking the blue and green hues of the painting.

BELOW Sweet locally grown strawberries and a milkshake make an accidentally coordinated snack to enjoy in this red-and-white themed house.

BRIDGEHAMPTON COTTAGE

SANDWICHED BETWEEN THE EASTERN SEABOARD AND THE SMALL VILLAGE OF BRIDGEHAMPTON, WHOSE MAIN STREET IS LINED WITH BOUTIQUES COVERED WITH TWINKLING FAIRY LIGHTS, BAKERIES, AND FINE RESTAURANTS, THIS COTTAGE IS A PERFECT DESTINATION FOR A BUSY NEW YORKER TO ESCAPE TO FOR LONG WEEKENDS AND VACATIONS.

As a buyer of rare antiques and collectables, the owner of this whitewashed weatherboard home has created a perfectly coordinated treasure trove of vintage finds. Robust, timeworn fabrics are a recurring feature of the interior, and her eye for tones and shades, interesting textures, and unusual materials are evident. The splash of color provided by the retro school chairs, vintage

LEFT The occasional rumbling of a freight train gently sloping along the track that runs behind the fence is not a nuisance, but a reassurance that all is well in the outside world. The weather-worn Adirondack chairs, made comfortable with large cushions in a raspberry toile design, are in a perfect spot to take in the sun and the views across the meadow in front of the house. The table is prettily dressed with a well-loved casually crumpled pink cloth, topped by a simple runner of antique linen and enamel pitchers. The advantage of using linens is the resilience of the fabric, and the fact that the aging process continues to add to its charm.

RIGHT The veranda encircling the entire house is simply furnished with vintage metal-work benches and understated pieces of outdoor furniture. It is carefully uncluttered, so that it can be cleared easily when winter comes to make room for neat stacks of firewood. A bundle of kindling makes a rustic decoration until it is put to use.

patterned curtains, and strongly striped cushions and pillows, covered in antique linen hand-printed in England, is welcome in the simple white kitchen, with its generously sized old painted table and floorboards. This informal dining area can be dressed up with large bunches of wild flowers and sturdy candles in oversized cylindrical glass vases—objects of art in their own right.

Many of the quirky and unusual pieces dotted about the house are leftover stock from the owner's antiques shop, now sadly closed, which add real points of interest and charm to the home. The normally clinical standards required by tenants are cast aside; the waiting list to rent this house is insatiable and is testament to her clever assemblage.

The light and airy sitting room has no television, thus encouraging the more wholesome aspects of life. Toile, floral, and wide-striped fabrics mix together comfortably. The collections of magazines and inspirational books on artists and design movements jostle for space on a large coffee table.

ABOVE A stock pile of *World of Interiors* magazines, accumulated over decades, towers on top of a charming antique stamp chest. An ornate Chinese lantern sits on a battered stool next to the working fire, which is laid ready for a chilly evening. A collection of old coral, predating the outlawing of its harvest, is displayed on the mantelpiece, together with pages from a 1920s science journal.

The whole property has been decorated and styled in a manner similar to shop merchandise, with the themes of reds, whites, faded linens, and French antique prints offset with old American utility-wear and driftwood-faded furniture. Nothing is out of place, yet the comfort of the Cabbages & Roses cushions, piles of vintage linens and cottons, and the stacks of design books on every available surface create a relaxed and homey environment.

The house has benefited from the occasional clearout, when unsuitable dust-gathering clutter was disposed of, allowing those possessions which are either of great sentimental value, or of colorful or practical merit, to find a new station in life. Gradually, over a period of two years or so, the red-and-

On the industrial table stands chipped
enamelware and a selection of gray and black
printed linens from Cabbages & Roses. The
small red ball of string ensures the display is
not alienated from the careful theme that
runs throughout the house.

ABOVE The vast expanse of old white wooden cupboards provide ample space for the necessities of the kitchen to be stowed neatly—well-displayed kitchenware is crucial if your cupboard doors are made from glass. The organization within the house is prevalent, but it is at its most apparent in this room. Items in frequent use can be stashed neatly in corners, with attractive retro goods such as the old silver kettle and bright dish cloths.

white theme has dominated the house, which was once enveloped in blue. All the blue possessions that were too precious to part with have found a new home in the garden outhouse, which is used as a spare room and studio, providing a secluded space in which to paint amid fond memories.

The living quarters are the main focus of the house, with the bedrooms and bathrooms accessed by two different staircases that lead up to the east and west wings and the turret-like additions to each side of the building. Everything leads down to the living rooms and kitchen, enticing the congregation of guests to the most comfortable and sociable areas.

The kitchen occupies the central core of the interior, with its imposing custom-made glass cabinets and generous storage space hidden behind

ABOVE The huge collection of tableware, gathered over a lifetime, is proudly presented in haphazard piles, but the coordination of color and style keeps it looking ordered.

painted wooden doors. The items stored in the glass-fronted cupboards have been accumulated over the years, and the impressive tableware collection makes a calm and utilitarian display. There is a wealth of giant bowls and industrial-sized shiny silver pots and pans ready and waiting for the next long lunch in the garden or supper party at the large table overlooking the veranda and garden beyond.

Here and there, the bright packaging of perishables that have crept beyond the boundaries of the large pantry and laundry room next door add unexpected dashes of color. It is a kitchen large enough to entertain all the house's inhabitants and encourages everyone to participate in the social process of food preparation.

FAR LEFT An antique statue of a jockey sits on a spare spot on the veranda that surrounds the house. The flaking paint adds to his charm, and one wonders how or why he came about.

LEFT An example of the owner's attention to detail and eye for a tableau, a radiator in one of the corridors is decorated with a pile of pebbles from the local beach and some old button boxes that are perfectly in tune with the neutral theme.

The creator of this home is a true stylist. Wandering around the house, you stumble upon the most intricate displays—small collections made up of some surprisingly resourceful and unusual items that form miniature art installations—which are there one day and then reshuffled, rearranged, and redistributed to an area that she feels is slightly lacking. It is a privilege to be party to this type of fluid creativity, making you vow to go home and try out similar things—from placing a charming figurine in an empty corner in the garden, to perching a simple vase of flowers on a hallway floor, to stacking up a vast collection of magazines, which not only provides glossy pages of rich inspiration, but forms a towering white sculpture to sit alongside finds from the Far East.

Impeccable taste is adhered to without compromise. Even the everyday fittings and architectural details of radiators and other necessary working objects are manipulated to fit into the whole scene of a room.

The main elements of the house, the faded and chipped white-painted furniture and neutral backgrounds

THE GARDEN IS ONE OF THE MANY PLEASURES THAT COME WITH THE HOUSE, AND VISITORS DELIGHT IN THE OUTHOUSES AND THE VERANDA THAT ENCIRCLES THE ENTIRE BUILDING UNDER COVER FROM THE OVERHANGING ROOF.

ABOVE An amalgamation of vintage articles are carefully placed on top of an old stamp chest to make an impromptu still life. The unpainted mirror frame makes a strong statement against the softer fabrics, flaking paint, and shades of white elsewhere in the room.

and floors, are consistent throughout, so that once the next palette has been chosen, the heavenly task of trawling favorite antiques markets and vintage shops for a new collection to fill the perfect canvas can begin again.

ABOVE The bathroom has been furnished with a tub that sits perfectly inside the turret-shaped window alcove. The simple lines and tones of the minimal furniture create a sense of purity and cleanliness.

OPPOSITE, TOP Quaint gingham Roman blinds brighten up the private study area, which is isolated from the rest of the house to provide a sanctuary where tasks can be focused on uninterrupted.

OPPOSITE, BOTTOM The vintage red dress hanging at the top of the secret stairs breaks up the mass of white woodwork that prevails around the house.

The staircases in this tardis-like house lead up to two slightly irregular turrets, which are flooded with natural light streaming in through the wall of windows under simple Roman blinds. The main bedroom is open to its turret, which has been turned into a vantage point with far-reaching views over the countryside. The other turret is used as a bathroom for the bedroom that adjoins it. The deep roll-top bathtub is perfectly positioned under the windows to give a view of the surrounding treetops.

A tiny wooden staircase leads up past a charming vintage red check dress to a guest room and study. This room is a sanctuary, made more so by the feeling of secrecy engendered by the private stairs. Like a doll's house, it is

decorated with tiny ballerina shoes, exquisite antique lace undergarments, and a collection of antique slippers, all picked for their beauty, rich embroidery, and tone—a homage to the beauty of old-fashioned craftsmanship. It is good to appreciate the importance of specialized skills and the careful custodianship of one-off pieces that have lasted hundreds of years, as these have. Stashes of old papers and inspirational notes and pictures are neatly stored away, protecting them from sun damage inside old-fashioned trunks, suitcases, and box files. The whole house appears to cherish and recycle pieces of well-loved history, and it is this sense of anti-consumerism that adds an intricate depth to the relatively new home.

THE WHOLE HOUSE IS A TREASURE TROVE OF
QUIRKY ANTIQUES AND DISPLAYS OF WELL-LOVED
OBJECTS, WHICH ARE FREQUENTLY REARRANGED
INTO NEW VIGNETTES TO KEEP THINGS FRESH
AND INTERESTING.

The comfort of this room is enveloping and
almost immediately becomes your own. The
matte black metallic bed frame and table
base work well with the dark portrait
watching over the room and have given it
a sophisticated European mood, with the
blacks drawing on the brightness of the reds
in the pillowcases and vintage toile de Jouy
quilt. On the bedside table are small piles
of well-chosen books and treasures to
dwell on as you drift off to sleep in the
softness of the layered cottons.

ABOVE For someone who appreciates hearing the wildlife in the garden, this studio outhouse, an overflow to the main house, is the perfect retreat. A hotchpotch of vintage blue fabrics sit happily with a Cabbages & Roses floral print cushion, and the fine paintings add a seriousness to the scene.

RIGHT An old hospital table has been reinvented and is often used for breakfast in bed. Gingham blinds allow morning light to stream into the room, and pillows in similar checked fabric mix well with Cabbages & Roses bed linen in various prints.

63

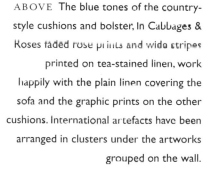

LOFT LIVING

CREATING A COMFORTABLE HOME WITHIN A VAST SPACE IS NOT AS EASY AS THIS NEW YORK LOFT APARTMENT WOULD ALLOW YOU TO BELIEVE. PROPORTIONALLY, THE FURNITURE HAS TO MATCH THE SPACE IT FINDS ITSELF IN. THERE IS ALSO THE TEMPTATION TO FILL ALL THE SPACE YOU HAVE, BUT ENVIRONMENTS SUCH AS THIS CAN BE UNFORGIVING IF THEY BECOME DELUGED IN CLUTTER. THE KEY TO SUCCESS IS BRUTAL SELECTION, SO THE PERFECT SPACE CAN BE A LONG TIME IN THE MAKING.

ABOVE The blue tones of the country-style cushions and bolster, In Cabbages & Roses faded rose prints and wide stripes printed on tea-stained linen, work happily with the plain linen covering the sofa and the graphic prints on the other cushions. International artefacts have been arranged in clusters under the artworks grouped on the wall.

OPPOSITE Tall windows allow light to stream into the apartment and the high ceilings make the space seem huge and airy. The modern pictures—a mix of prints, photographs, and paintings—are elegantly hung, either surrounded by wall space to let them breathe or hung in groups for impact. The large Hentie van der Merwe painting takes pride of place.

RIGHT Bookcases are put to good use throughout the apartment, decluttering the surfaces but creating interest with the neatly stowed possessions.

Every aspect of this apartment has been carefully curated. Bespoke furniture bridges the gap between functional everyday necessities and the artwork arranged on the walls. Oversized pieces mimic the scale and style of the original features of the pre-war industrial building, drawing the eye to those focal points. Texture and tone are used to great effect to cordon off the various zones within the large open-plan space; the use of wood and well-worn leather gives a tougher edge to soft printed linens, which are further contrasted with strong modern prints on the plain sofa. The textures of the cowhide against the wood floor, the metal sofa legs spiking out of the linen upholstery, and the large lamp in front of the tall window are the juxtapositions that create interest.

Contrast is the order of the day in this interesting,
comfortable living room. Old blends with new; the
serious is offset by humor; religious statues sit next to
retro pieces; and the softer vibe of the Cabbages & Roses
florals adds restraint to the scene.

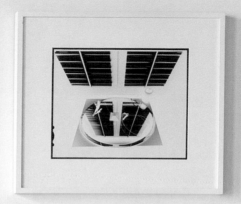

The witty and offbeat themes that run through the apartment are continued in the main bedroom. A relaxing haven away from all the city bustle and family life, it is decorated with monotone family photos from the 1940s and edgy anatomical prints of skulls, rudimentary Mexican paintings, and blackened crucifixes. The calming atmosphere of the room stems from the simplicity of the color scheme and pieces of furniture. It is easy to create a bland minimal space, but the balance here has been achieved through the use of bold black lines set against the whiteness of the walls. There is no fuss or frill, and interest is added by imperfection—be it a rough wooden surface or an amalgamation of mismatched pictures and chipped glass ornaments.

The main living space has an exposed brickwork wall running the whole length of the room, adding warmth and texture to counter the plain plaster evident elsewhere in the apartment. The flexible dining room-cum-spare room is drawn into its own space not by solid walls, but by an L-shaped curtain that encloses a private area when required, shutting off the industrial-style kitchen from a dinner party, or enclosing a guest in a clandestine tent-like linen and brick room. This is an exemplary way to achieve the flexible space that is so popular in crowded cities and is perfect for lofts where the open-plan rooms can remain intact, but also be fully utilized when needed.

ABOVE AND OPPOSITE The haphazard hanging of mismatched frames and images creates interest on the otherwise bare bedroom walls. Understated furniture and uncrowded collections allow the space to feel organized and calm. Small vases holding flower heads are scattered about for a softening touch—a different style and color of flower could be used to change the whole theme of the room.

WHILE THE POSSESSIONS ON DISPLAY ARE MINIMAL AND
WELL-CHOSEN, THEY ARE GROUPED TOGETHER TO MAKE MAXIMUM
IMPACT ON THE EMPTY WHITE SPACE THE WALL PROVIDES.

OPPOSITE AND ABOVE In an open-plan layout, simple linen curtains are a great way to zone off an area and provide a level of privacy when required, without compromising the quality of the space. In the main living area, warmth and interest is supplied by original features such as the exposed brickwork and wooden beams. In the dining area, chair covers made up from scraps of different Cabbages & Roses fabrics keep the mood informal. A clever way to make smaller pieces of furniture appear larger is to hang pictures on the wall just above them, adding height to the overall scene.

Separate zones and individual spaces are created throughout the apartment by angling the furniture, creating nonparallel lines that provide partial alcoves within the large rectangular room. Each hub forms a scene, in keeping with the rest of the room but showcasing specific collections, like all the family photo albums stored on a bookcase next to a comfy two-seater chair, or the complete collection of Buildings of Disaster below quirky Mexican folk figurines.

The modernity of the apartment has been taken seriously, and this has infiltrated into the structure. Smart, inconspicuous radiators encircle the room without imposing on their surroundings. Functionality is hidden well—stereos and thermostats are concealed, light switches are handsome and of fine quality. Nothing is done half-heartedly, and it is the little things that make a significant difference when so much of the house is on display, proving that the real talent in renovating a loft space is in having the staying power to do it from beginning to end without compromise.

The bedroom quarters are kept simple and neat. The children's room is furnished with ingenious storage

OPPOSITE The clever placement of furniture and lighting can be used to create individual areas within an open space. Here, a cozy corner for reading or looking through collections of photographs is formed by positioning a large armchair at an angle in front of a window and bookshelf, with a lamp on the table next to it. Modern pieces of furniture are played against groups of old Mexican figures.

solutions, including a magnetic strip that encircles the room allowing paintings and keepsakes to be displayed on the walls, and built-in boxes for clothes and toys. The relatively small space, which contains two beds, thus remains uncluttered and easy to keep tidy. The bright colors of the American flag recur across the room in the striped bed linen and patterned cushions and pillows.

The master bedroom is a massive space with very little furniture. Personal collections, pictures, and books are housed on shelves or hung on the walls, allowing the floor to remain uncluttered and calm. The use of sheer white muslin as a window dressing softens the light that streams through the bedroom windows and blurs the urban landscape outside and the billboards seen on the streets below. It also provides privacy from the opposite neighbors, while letting in as much natural light as if the windows were bare.

THE LACK OF STORAGE SPACE HAS PROMPTED THE MANIPULATION OF PERSONAL POSSESSIONS INTO ATTRACTIVE DISPLAYS, ON THE WALLS AND ON THE OPEN BOOKSHELVES THAT FILL IN AWKWARD CORNER CAVITIES.

ABOVE The main bedroom is kept very simple and personal. A splash of color from the duvet cover and posy of fresh roses is just enough to bring the feeling of spring to the room.

LEFT The children's bedroom is kept organized with plenty of hidden storage and a simple color scheme. The accessories, cushions, and bed linen are easy to update with the children's ever-changing tastes and passions.

STUDIO APARTMENT

THIS SMART, COMPACT APARTMENT IS THE NEW YORK EQUIVALENT TO A CROW'S NEST, OVERLOOKING A BUSY COMMUTER STREET IN UPTOWN MANHATTAN. IN AN EMINENTLY DESIRABLE AND LIVELY CITY SUCH AS THIS, WHERE LIVING SPACE IS AT A PREMIUM, CLEVER DESIGN IS KEY.

Here, the limited space available has been ingeniously adapted to make use of every square foot. What appears at first glance to be a wall is, in fact, a row of large walk-in closets. The kitchen, too, is no more than a small cupboard cleverly designed to incorporate all you need to cook and entertain. Even

OPPOSITE The design of this apartment is based on optical illusions and clever visual tricks that give the appearance of more space. The height of the ceiling, tall windows, and use of large mirrors all enhance the sense of volume. Keeping the color palette and contents uniform and less complex minimizes the negative effects of clutter that could result when storage and square footage are limited. The grays and charcoals of the furniture blend with the color scheme of the room, almost shifting it outward to merge with the walls.

ABOVE A walk-in cupboard has been redesigned to form a kitchen, with concealed storage extending as high as possible to accommodate all the tools. The glassware and crockery make an attractive display—a clever solution in a multi-functional space.

the study is hidden behind a double-height door leading off the main sitting area. Adjustable and foldaway furniture, such as the dining table, allows the freedom of choosing to utilize the space for specific purposes.

Throughout the apartment, monochrome décor has been used to promote a feeling of calm and order. In addition, the masculine black upholstery acts as an interior slimming aid, making the furniture in the living area appear less dominant.

The most has been made of the tall ceilings and windows to enhance the sense of volume within the apartment. In the sophisticated entrance hall, wood paneling reaching up to the ceiling

The neutral linens used in the bedroom creates a comfortable sanctuary above the hectic streets of Manhattan. Ensuring that everything is of similar tones means that different patterns and plains can be mixed together on pillows and cushions of various shapes and sizes. Complementary Cabbages & Roses box files are perfect for stowing away anything unappealing or unsightly.

accentuates the height of the walls and adds a touch of grandeur. The floor-to-ceiling windows support the feeling of space and airiness, and the proportions of the steep staircase leading up to the sleeping area deceive you into believing you are looking at a wider space.

The mezzanine bedroom at the top of the skinny staircase also illustrates the ingenious design and clever use of space—achieving privacy from the main living area while making the most of its height. The furnishings from Cabbages & Roses' Langton range give an edgy androgynous warmth, which could be transformed entirely, simply by swapping the bedcover to create a romantic feminine boudoir.

OPPOSITE The top deck of the houseboat can serve as many things—a dining room with a great river view, or a perfect suntrap for an afternoon siesta, with a refreshing breeze and the activity of the River Thames floating by.

RIGHT Monotone shopping bags are kept near the entrance to the kitchen to ensure they will not be forgotten when going ashore to replenish supplies. They also add a decorative touch, breaking up the solid wood walls.

THE
HOUSEBOAT

HOUSEBOATS OFTEN MAKE ME THINK OF A SLIGHTLY MUSTY CANAL BOAT CRUISING THE WATERWAYS THAT CRISSCROSS THE BRITISH COUNTRYSIDE. THAT WAS UNTIL I SAW THIS STATE-OF-THE-ART HOUSEBOAT MOORED IN CENTRAL LONDON. THE OWNERS COMMISSIONED WEST COUNTRY BOAT-BUILDER WILLIAM TRICKETT TO BUILD THEM A SEAFARING BARGE WITH SUCH HIGH SPECIFICATIONS THAT IT TOOK ALL OF THREE YEARS TO BUILD. THE EXPERTLY CRAFTED OAK BOAT, NAMED AFTER THE OWNERS' TWO DAUGHTERS, WAS FINALLY LAUNCHED IN THE NOTORIOUSLY WET SUMMER OF 2008.

LEFT The kitchen is kept bright and vibrant with the use of color and rich textures. Everything has its place and can be stowed away securely and neatly in anticipation of a choppy day on the river. Its vibrancy comes from the deep, rich velvets, while the old-fashioned floral print balances the kitchen's modern feel.

OPPOSITE The surprisingly large lower deck has the feel of an open-plan apartment, with the different living areas defined by subtle variations in the oak paneling. Looking through to the master cabin, the fine marquetry sun, with each sunbeam minutely carved and inlaid, serves both as a piece of art and as a substantial wall to ensure privacy in the bathroom. Decoration is unfussy and comfort is a priority.

This modern boat contains an important part of British history—a section of oak decking salvaged from the Cutty Sark, the nineteenth-century tea clipper that tragically caught fire in 2007 while being restored in a London dock.

Instead of making the usual decision to have a small apartment in London to use when visiting and working there, the owners decided to take the more challenging route of building their own "pied a l'eau" and finding a convenient mooring on the River Thames in central London. The result is a perfect hidey-hole in which to retreat from the busy city streets. In the summer, the roof deck and river breeze provide a much more refreshing alterative to the average city garden, and the eco-friendly heating system ensures that the boat is warm in the winter. The surprising space and carefully considered interior leave the family wanting for nothing.

The vast expanses of sustainable European oak, carved and polished and with finely carved marquetry, instantly warm the carefully organized and rather minimal setting. A welcoming, cozy feel is established by the use of comfortable cushions and soft fabrics in classic faded florals and plain colored velvets.

THE CARVED AND POLISHED WOOD USED THROUGHOUT THE INTERIOR OF THE
BOAT ADDS WARMTH TO THE OTHERWISE MINIMAL SETTING.

The upstairs deck is the notorious location of the fantastical dinner parties the owners like to host, but it is also refined enough to be able to serve as a spare bedroom, sun deck, and, most importantly, captain's navigation center, complete with high-tech equipment. The nautical and patriotic reds, whites, and blues used in the furnishings bring a jolly theme to the deck, and the bold contrasts around the room create a lively atmosphere without the clutter of decorative objects. A mix of bold stripes, monotone florals, and simple plain fabrics create an interesting but informal look. Soft linens against the harsh lines of the steel and wood ensure a comfortable environment, even on a working vessel.

One of the most important aspects of boat design is the care and attention paid to the functionality of space. The layout needs to be uncluttered to allow ease

FAR LEFT Every inch of space is utilized. In the corridor leading upstairs, the black-and-white check curtain accentuates the split of different zones within the boat without taking up the space a door would require.

LEFT The perfectly ordered bathroom is both brilliantly functional and stylish. A luxurious element is added by the stacks of soft towels and indulgent bathroom products.

OPPOSITE The simplicity of the fabric used for the bed cover enables the patterns to stand out and enhance the surroundings, while not overwhelming the dramatic woodwork. A glimpse into the cocoon-like main cabin shows an immaculate and restful place.

of movement from one area to another, with clearly defined zones and space-saving furniture and fittings. The owners have followed these principles when it comes to the boat's internal furnishings, finding unusual pieces which are useful and necessary but that pull the interior together in a restrained way. The design leaves space for this creative and energetic family to do their own thing unhindered in a comparatively small space.

Throughout the boat, fabrics and possessions are used cleverly to break up the broad sweep of oak. The owners have worked hard to enhance and highlight the striking craftsmanship that is evident at every turn,

taking advantage of the grains and natural markings of the wood and using very simple elements to bring it all together and create a home. Cabbages & Roses' Langton range of grays, blacks, and natural linens subtly enhances the lower deck and cabins.

The barge has journeyed around the UK's inland waterways, and plans are afoot to traverse the high seas, but for now it makes a very comfortable waterside home. The houseboat was created by the whole family, and their various personalities shine though in every part. It has evolved to be the perfect fit for them, and an absolute joy to visit.

Island Country

CAPE COD

ON THE EAST COAST OF AMERICA, ALMOST DIPPING ITS TOE INTO THE WILD ATLANTIC OCEAN, IS A GREAT EXAMPLE OF SIMPLE VERNACULAR BEACHSIDE ARCHITECTURE. BUILT BY ITS OWNERS 15 YEARS AGO, THE HOUSE HAS SETTLED INTO ITS SURROUNDINGS AS COMFORTABLY AS ITS INHABITANTS HAVE SETTLED INTO IT. THE HOUSE HAS A TREMENDOUS AMOUNT OF SPACE, WITH A LARGE OPEN-PLAN LIVING AREA ON THE GROUND FLOOR AND A GARDEN WITH A TENNIS COURT LEADING DOWN TO THE BEACH, GIVING THE IMPRESSION THAT THE BOUNDARY STRETCHES RIGHT OUT TO THE HORIZON AT THE EDGE OF THE OCEAN.

OPPOSITE The beautiful house looks as if it has been there for hundreds of years, not a mere 15. An osprey with extreme good taste has set up home above the rough grassy area, with a fine view of the property.

RIGHT The bold red stripes on the cushion give a burst of solid color to this charming vignette, with the cast-off running shoes casually left alongside the weather-worn painted bench and galvanized tub.

ABOVE LEFT The house is a stone's throw away from the beach, which, like all Cape Cod beaches, is delightfully wild and unkempt—romantic in the extreme.

ABOVE The veranda surrounding the entire house makes the most of the sunshine and ocean views. Cabbages & Roses furnishings add a touch of English country style.

OPPOSITE LEFT Subdued colors and a mix of plain and patterned linens are all that is needed in this airy room—the varying shades of white and cream make it feel both warm and light.

OPPOSITE, TOP AND BOTTOM RIGHT Every aspect of the house has been designed to accommodate the lifestyle of the people who live there, with plenty of space created to show off their extensive collections of glass, china, and silver. With its generous open shelves, the larder is the perfect spot to showcase some of the finds from local antique fairs.

This house is a full-time home, so there is no need for the storage areas required by many of its neighboring properties to keep precious or personal items, and bulky belongings such as wetsuits and surfboards, hidden from tenants. Nevertheless, this is a practical beachside house, with hard-wearing furnishings and wooden floorboards downstairs, making it easy to sweep up the sand that sneaks inside between toes, with generous rugs added for warmth in the winter months.

The airy living space unfolds from the main entrance at the center of the house, with split levels separating the relaxation areas from the working areas. The lack of curtains, blinds, or shades is compensated for by the comfortable interior, and means that it is always possible to look out at the array of multicolored birds drawn to the rockery garden and bird tables outside.

ABOVE A seaside home cannot afford to be too precious. The décor needs to be able to withstand the wear and tear of relaxed living, where sand can be trampled over the floors and easily swept up, and salty pets can curl up on linen and cotton furnishings that are hard-wearing and easy to wash.

The sitting room is simply furnished with natural materials and textures. Flourishes of color are added in the form of vintage linen cushions and a smattering of printed Cabbages & Roses fabrics in toning shades. In a neutral interior, these subtle prints make adaptable base cloths, allowing new themes to be introduced by the change of a cushion or throw. Beautifully arranged collections of china and glass, sourced from local antique fairs, are displayed on shelves. The relaxed atmosphere invites you to curl up and admire the views through the rows of large windows encircling each room. The second sitting room, also surrounded by bay windows,

is a celebration of the outdoors. Tables are laden with displays of shells, and an old-fashioned telescope brings distant nature indoors.

The main entertaining space faces the sea, and the view is the undisputed focal point of the room. Embellishments are basic, the chairs are kept uniform with simple linen slipcovers, and unlined curtains have a mellowing effect on the light reflecting off the ocean. In the winter months, when friends come to visit the deserted beaches for a long weekend, conversation draws out over lengthy dinners with the backdrop of stormy ocean waves crashing on the shore outside. The neutral décor lends itself to the flexibility needed to create different scenes at the drop of a tablecloth.

With versatile neutral décor as a backdrop, the dining area can be dressed up or down as the occasion and season demands. The flatware, fine bone china, and glassware, along with the collections of sun-bleached shells and other decorations dotted about the room, are all able to work themselves into whichever scheme or color theme suits the prevailing mood.

The private quarters upstairs are spacious and simple, with large pieces of heavy vintage furniture acting as the focal point around which each room has evolved. Dark wood pieces smarten up the whitewashed walls and wooden shutters. This gives the option to play up to the formality of a four-poster bed and matching furniture, or to play it down with warm carpet, rugs, or natural floor coverings and colors suggested by one of the seashore oil paintings collected over the years. The rooms show a brave cross-section of design periods and style: Art Deco items befriend contemporary tones while holding their own against an abruptly puritan Victorian piece.

Through the upstairs of the house there is a fusion of contemporary and vintage pieces. Comfort is never

THE GENEROUS SIZE OF THE FURNITURE PERFORMS A ROLE OF GRANDEUR, WHICH IS BALANCED BY THE GROUNDING COMFORT OF AGE AND TEXTURE.

OPPOSITE The imposing four-poster bed, dressed elegantly with only a touch of pattern, is undoubtedly the star piece of this large, sophisticated bedroom. The décor is kept very simple, with whitewashed walls and a natural-fiber rug on the polished wood floor.

ABOVE RIGHT Taking inspiration from the different shades of blue in the seascape paintings, the bed is dressed with a comfortable mix of old and new bed linens in floral prints, stripes, and crisp plain white, topped with a striped pillow made from an antique linen sheet.

compromised; new bed linen is topped with vintage quilts, throws, and pillows, each chosen for an element of its character, whether it's the blue stripe of an antique linen sheet, or mismatched bed linen chosen for its tones.

Despite the house being so large, it has only three bedrooms. Being built with the sea and ensuing lifestyle in mind, instead of a fourth bedroom there is an airy landing leading to a roof deck, where the natural beauty and sea breeze can be fully appreciated.

A plump print cushion sits unobtrusively within the scheme of dark wood flooring and clean white lines. On the mantelpiece is part of the vast and impressive collection of pure white Wedgwood china, which is displayed to great effect all around the house. The wire basket filled with pieces of driftwood and the antique steel fire tools propped up against the fire surround perfectly complement the calm scene with their rich variety of textures and natural tones—a great example of beautiful as well as necessary items, used as much for decoration as for keeping warm.

LONG ISLAND

In New York state, just east of Manhattan, Long Island stretches northward into the Atlantic Ocean, connected to the city by several bridges and tunnels. The western side of the island was once a Dutch colony, but in 1664 it was taken over by the English, who had originally settled on the eastern side. The architectural legacy of both countries is what makes Long Island the desirable place it is today.

A peaceful refuge from city life, this house, which was built in 1720—making it old as far as American architecture is concerned—emerges from a group of barns and outhouses. The old buildings have been made into a luxurious home; a comfortable, calm retreat, which has been gradually and sympathetically restored over the years, with the last renovation completed in 2002. The current project is the restoration of an old boathouse by the Carmans River, which flows along the edge of the property and runs out to sea at Smith Point, a national park by the ocean, a mere 20 minutes' drive away.

The property comprises many old outbuildings, each serving their own unique purpose. A hut nestling beside the Carmans River, for example, has been transformed into a small guest dwelling, set apart from the main house and so in relative privacy. The tiny shed has been kept as an old-fashioned outdoor lavatory, preserving some of the history and memory of the original dwelling. Clad in traditional wood weatherboarding, and of course painted white, the shed has not escaped the designer's finishing touch—the carriage lantern artfully placed at the door, giving this usually inconsequential facility a touch of class. It is to the credit of the designer that hundreds of years and many owners later, the care and pride taken to build this house are still apparent in the original details that have been preserved so beautifully.

The typical Long Island palette of off-white paint and weathered, faded gray wood works perfectly with the sympathetic and discerning use of color at play within the buildings. The shades of white and soft gray-greens, the

OPPOSITE, TOP The sheds in the garden each have their own personality, with cozy guest rooms decorated with carefully chosen linens and cushions to welcome you inside. Each hut has a small lantern to guide you from place to place in the darkness.

OPPOSITE, BOTTOM Plenty of hand-crafted details can be found around the outside of the main house and outhouses, preserved in appreciation of the artisans who carved them hundreds of years ago.

BELOW The front of the house belies the spaciousness of its interior, but is perfectly in keeping with the understated design within.

metals, and the natural wood all create a sophisticated, restrained country feel, while retaining the elements of nature and the patina of wear and tear developed through many years of use.

As part of a continuing river community, the local town, and indeed the whole area, has managed to stave off much of the negativity that so many rural and historic towns and villages have encountered with their modernization and development. The sense of protection and care is apparent throughout the locality: its inhabitants are warm and friendly, watching out for each other and regularly organizing get-togethers to keep abreast of the town's goings-on.

The porch at the back of the house provides a sheltered platform with views of the garden. An old-fashioned bathing tub makes an ideal weatherproof container for kindling wood and fire logs; it is topped up regularly with fallen branches from around the garden, but also fed weekly during the winter months by local deliveries. The white paintwork and old wooden furniture together make a calm and beautiful refuge, with a touch of comfort added by the cushion, whose cool pale gray tones complete the restful scene.

ABOVE The plume of soot that has gradually escaped from the fireplace and darkened the white wall above it has become a true focal point of the kitchen, and almost a piece of art in its celebration of nature and natural form. There is very little color in the room, and the simple white backdrop brings out the beauty of the plants and old terracotta pots on the dining table. The cushions provide comfort and pattern in a subtle and unassuming way.

Time has been taken in the creation of every facet of this home and every detail has been well considered. Hidden sound systems, with no visible tangle of leads, and purpose-built storage spaces strategically hide the unsightly facts of life, while the more decorative contents of the house are on display.

The kitchen is a basic and unembellished room, but no compromise has been made in its creation. Everything has been carefully selected, not just for its usefulness, but for its value within the composition of the entire scheme. Intrinsic beauty has been found in the soot deposits that have accumulated over the years from the smoking fire, relinquishing the need to add anything else to the wall in this otherwise immaculate white room. The warm tone

RIGHT Here is a perfect example of the joy one can have in carefully staging precious keepsakes and using them as a display. This charming arrangement is composed of finds gathered from the beach and local markets, and aged books, whose pale, timeworn colors draw the collection together.

THE FUNCTIONALITY OF THE HOUSE IS MAPPED AND ESTABLISHED, ALLOWING A FREE REIN TO EMBELLISH WITH ARTISTIC FLAIR, USING COLLECTIONS OF SHELLS, BOOKS, AND ENCHANTING PIECES OF CHINA.

and rough texture of the weathered terracotta pots add a natural touch, which softens the minimalist blow. The simplicity of the interior design would not tolerate the clutter of unnecessary objects and brings out the beauty in the carefully selected pieces that remain on show. This way of decorating enables an easily changeable canvas—a new centerpiece is all that is required to completely alter the perspective and mood of a room.

What makes an interior feel homey, enchanting, and welcoming are the personal touches—cushions and pillows, tablecloths, collections, and antique finds—that express the personality of the occupants and convey their interests. The neutral and well-considered foundations of this interior allow for the addition of monotone or colored accents, modern or antique pieces with equal flexibility, allowing the owners to add the things they truly love, rather than those that are considered fashionable. The rare find of a whole set of matching vintage dining chairs demonstrates a type of patience that comes with being a discerning and determined homemaker.

In the formal sitting room, the worn dark wood flooring grounds the airy whites and creams, and modern sofas are juxtaposed against antique finds. Both the sofa and an old winged armchair are covered with the same loose-fitting off-white linen. The off-black prints on the aged-gray linen sit happily beside the heavily textured Indian cushion, fusing two very different cultures that are renowned for their appreciation of fabric and texture. Glass and ceramic objects harden the soft edges of the comfort zone, adding sophistication without fuss. The simple half shutters allow natural light into the room, but preserve the privacy of its occupants.

The relaxed unlined linen shade allows enough light through the window while maintaining privacy. At night, the candles in the wrought-iron chandelier are lit, casting a warm glow over this tranquil setting. The polished dark wood sideboard provides a strong backdrop for the collection of white Wedgwood china. The repetition of shape and style in the china collection retains the feeling of simplicity despite the generous clutter, while the mismatched sparkling glasses reinforce the informal vibe.

FURNISHING A HOME WITH ACCESSIBLE AND USEFUL OBJECTS IS A TRUE ARTFORM, BUT, WITH THOUGHT, EVERYDAY ITEMS CAN PRODUCE A DISPLAY THAT IS JUST AS EFFECTIVE AS PRICELESS PAINTINGS OR ARTEFACTS.

A recurring theme throughout the house revolves around the juxtaposition of dark wood flooring and heavy furniture with the neutral off-white tones of the walls, soft furnishings, white-painted furniture, and decorative objects. The result is an elegant, composed, and serene home, the lines, shapes, and varying textures perfectly silhouetted against the aged wood. The space relies heavily on the use of textured linens, woolen throws, and monotone patterns to provide an injection of comfort and color, which reinforce a feeling of homeliness and personality within the rooms.

In the upstairs quarters, there are further collections and unexpected treasures on display. As in all good houses, it is the eccentric knickknacks that say so much about the owner. In this case, the collections all seem so suited to the space they find themselves in because they have been worked into the scheme at the outset and have become the essence of the house. Often the trick to creating a pleasing display lies in the repetition of similar objects, or the grouping of items of a similar material and color.

It is clear that the owner of this home delights in simple, beautiful objects, and it is a good lesson to learn that these can happily take the place of walls crammed with fine artwork or cabinets groaning with priceless ornaments. In the bathroom, for example, a huge pile of towels and collection of unusual woven slippers prove that even the most basic and everyday objects can (and should) be as beautiful as any work of art. In sharp contrast to these soft and rustic textures are the austere slate floor and clinical white bathroom fittings. The only touch of pattern and color is brought into the mix by the printed bag hanging casually on the doorknob, which adds another element of softness and warmth. The combination of tones and textures creates a bathroom with the perfect balance of modern and old-fashioned style.

OPPOSITE The airy modern bathroom is kept looking timeless with classic shapes that have survived through the decades, such as the traditional claw-foot bathtub. A pedestal sink looks reassuringly sturdy, while the elegant oval mirror above it lends a simple beauty to the scene. The dark gray slate floor grounds the stark white fixtures and unadorned walls. Touches of texture are added in the form of the woven slippers, waffle bathmat, natural sponge, and printed linen bag.

LEFT Only carefully selected objects with special significance to the owner are kept on view in the master bedroom. A collection of vintage shoes lined up neatly on a small chest beside a hand-thrown bowl brings a sense of nostalgia and order to the room.

OPPOSITE The bedroom is a relaxing retreat, whose atmosphere of peace is enhanced by the minimal decoration and the dramatic contrast of the heavy dark wood furniture against the empty white walls and white-painted floor. The pretty floral pillowcase brings a feminine, summery feel.

The master bedroom shows the simple decorative style employed throughout in the house in its boldest form. Minimal and without distraction, with a perfect balance of light and dark, it is a room that has been specifically designed to escape to—a complete haven.

As elsewhere in the house, the objects on display have been carefully chosen, and are obviously things that have great sentimental value to the owners, such as the miniature collection of vintage children's shoes perched neatly on top of the chest of drawers, and the specially commissioned hand-thrown bowl.

The imposing sleigh bed and mahogany chest of drawers make a huge impact, but the whiteness and simplicity of the walls and floor prevent them from overwhelming their surroundings. Heavy pieces of furniture such as these need space around them,

becoming statements of contrast against the white walls. This room seems starkly modern, despite nothing in it being new. It is restrained and disciplined, at the same time comfortable and generous. The play of plain and gently faded floral bed linen adds depth to the otherwise neutral space and brings a light summery feel to the room, without disturbing the mood of serenity and peace.

THERE IS A TIMELESS BEAUTY TO THIS HOME, ESPECIALLY IN THE DETAILS, BOTH ARCHITECTURAL AND DECORATIVE; ITS MINIMALISM IS COMFORTABLE, NOT AUSTERE, AND IT FEELS COZY WITHOUT OBVIOUS COLOR.

The color in the guest bedroom is provided by the single pale blue wall and gently faded bed linen in a mixture of two complementary blue fabrics. The sparse but comfortable decoration makes a peaceful place to rest your head.

FAR LEFT AND LEFT The heated outside shower, open to the elements, is an invigorating and energizing treat that brings you closer to nature and ultimate relaxation on a sunny holiday. On a nearby corner of one of the many wood-clad buildings that make up the property is a large contemporary outside light, which mimics the shape of the shower head.

BELOW The main house, a converted wooden barn with a glazed front wall, is set within a large rambling garden surrounded by trees.

SAG HARBOR

SAG HARBOR, IN SUFFOLK COUNTY, LONG ISLAND, BETWEEN THE BORDERS OF EAST HAMPTON AND SOUTH HAMPTON, WAS ONCE A WHALING TOWN WHOSE ORIGINS DATE BACK TO 1703. THIS UNIQUE PROPERTY, COMPRISING AN OPEN-PLAN HOUSE AMONG A SPRAWLING ARRAY OF OUTBUILDINGS AND HUTS, SLOTS PERFECTLY INTO THE SPARSELY POPULATED NEIGHBORHOOD THAT IS JUST A SHORT DISTANCE FROM NEW YORK CITY.

OPPOSITE Unpainted wood paneling gives the interior warmth, while the knots and grains provide natural patterning. The simple wood theme extends to the home-crafted sofa, made comfortable with a deep navy-and-white striped mattress-like cushion and a selection of vintage striped and floral cushions for color and pattern.

Primarily used for vacations, this charming, sporadic house has become home to collections of souvenirs accumulated from local junk shops and around the world. A successful combination of kitsch and comfortable, the house is geared towards outdoor living, with plenty of luxury and shelter provided outside the main house.

OPPOSITE Sag Harbor is a thriving community of permanent residents, unlike its neighbor, the Hamptons, which is largely made up of weekenders and vacationers. The town is beautifully kept, with carefully tended lawns. This wood-clad house, with its vibrant display of seasonal flowers competing with the Stars and Stripes flag flying proudly beside the front door, is characteristic of many in the town.

ABOVE AND RIGHT On entering the town of Sag Harbor, we chanced upon this extraordinary house decorated with buoys. The neat white picket fence is a common feature of houses in the area.

THE LONG, STRAIGHT ROADS BEAR A RESEMBLANCE TO THOSE IN ANY OTHER TYPICAL AMERICAN SUBURB, BUT IT IS EVIDENT THAT A SIGNIFICANT PORTION OF THIS COMMUNITY HAS A CREATIVE STREAK— WHETHER THEY ARE ARTISTS, ACTORS, OR AVID COLLECTORS.

Sag Harbor is the quirky cousin of the Hamptons, the epitome of East Coast seaside living combined with the edginess of its seasonal commuters from New York City. The fine summers and close proximity to the sea bring an inevitable tide of visitors escaping the heavy humidity of the city, but there is also a strong local community that makes this a great place to visit all year round, especially in the winter when dramatic storms roll off the Atlantic Ocean. The town itself has a wealth of rich attractions to discover, which run far deeper than seasonal shops and eateries for tourists. The former whaling community is now home to a variety of independent shops selling unique hand-crafted pieces, an eclectic mix of junk shops, and an original 1930s cinema. The houses are well kept and cared for, many proudly flying Stars and Stripes flags over immaculate gardens and porches. Various high-profile residents have taken advantage of the more remote outskirts, where they are neither alone in the wilderness nor among the prying eyes of neighbors.

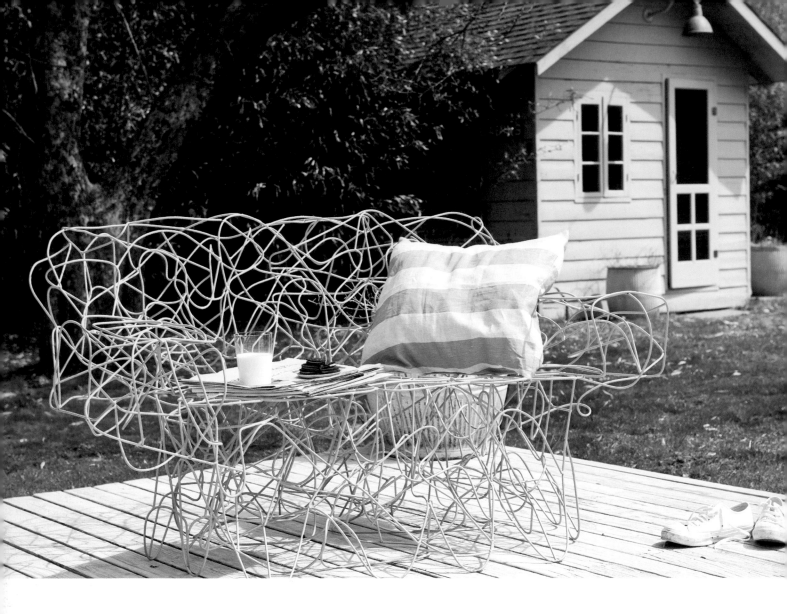

The main house is a very simple construction. It is, in effect, one large double-height open-plan barn space with sliding gauze partition walls that theoretically map out the different zones within the living space. A glazed wall lets in the sunlight and also encourages indoor life to spread towards the decking outside, which is furnished with unusual, sculptural wire garden furniture.

Like the interior, the garden is divided into different areas. This is achieved by the use of furniture as well as by the length of the grass and shrubbery, which is allowed to grow tall further away from the house, giving the impression of much wilder countryside than would normally be expected in a suburb. The pool area, in a field fenced off from the main garden, is wild and overgrown, enhancing the feeling of escapism when taking a dip. This private world, so far removed from urban impositions, is completely separate from the neat lawns and wood-clad outhouses lying beyond the fence.

OPPOSITE The modern wire furniture, standing on a stage of white-painted decking, is a work of art, made comfortable with the addition of a striped linen cushion. The little outhouse behind, one of many dotted about the garden, is used as a pool house.

ABOVE The black-and-white check tablecloth has a chic utilitarian feel, set off beautifully by the daffodils in their simple glass bottle.

ABOVE RIGHT A rustic folding table and wooden stools are ideal for an impromptu picnic or evening drink within the grassy wilderness. The tablecloth, cushion, and flowers make it more of a special event.

RIGHT Two charming weather-beaten wood chairs with a linen cushion make a restful area within the long grass.

We were thrilled to find a portrait of Elizabeth II, Queen of England, gracing the wall of this divine, eclectic house, which is furnished with a clever mix of contemporary and old pieces where nothing matches but everything is compatible. In a reverse of the norm, the ceiling is left as bare wood, while the walls are painted white, making a light but warm room. The sliding gauze door keeps natural light levels at a maximum, but creates a sense of separation when required.

The house's simple structure supports an uncluttered environment that allows the nineteenth-century antiques and 1920s paintings to present themselves in all their grandeur alongside other retro and vintage collectables. Each piece of the eclectic mix has found its own place and context within the series of spaces in the house and adjacent buildings, creating collections that seem to have gravitated together to produce different moods in areas of the house that serve different purposes. The pool house's alcove has evolved into a serious barbecue area, and the enjoyment to be had in eating is apparent in the paraphernalia that has amassed over the years. The stacks of easygoing colorful tableware give it a 1980s twist.

An eye for what works well in a space is what holds it all together and ensures it makes sense. The sleek lines and cool surfaces of the metallic kitchen are eased by the exposed wood frame of the ceiling and the wooden edging on the shelves that span a whole wall. Softer touches of linens and colorful old-fashioned kitchen appliances breathe some cheer and fun into the room.

OPPOSITE The display of kitchenware in the pool house alcove is as decorative as it is useful. The giant fish is a memento of the town's fishing heritage. The easy nature of the wood walls creates a warm, relaxed vibe.

ABOVE RIGHT Styles mix successfully here, with a battered office chair, classic desk, and display of lively artworks coming together to create a contemporary scene.

AN AMALGAMATION OF COLLECTABLES THAT SPAN THE DECADES HAVE ALL FOUND THEIR PLACE WITHIN THE SPRAWLING LAYOUT OF THE COMPLEX OF BUILDINGS, CREATING A SERIES OF UNIQUE SPACES.

LEFT The lovely retro kitchen is clean, spacious, and airy, with a clever mix of contemporary and vintage furnishings and paraphernalia. The interesting layout, with plenty of work spaces and seating, make this kitchen inviting and appealing. The unpainted ceiling with exposed beams is a theme running throughout the house, giving a feeling of space, even in the smaller rooms. The artwork throughout the property is very diverse, but it works together in an eclectic assembly. The bright orange coffee maker is a solitary block of color in an otherwise monotone scheme.

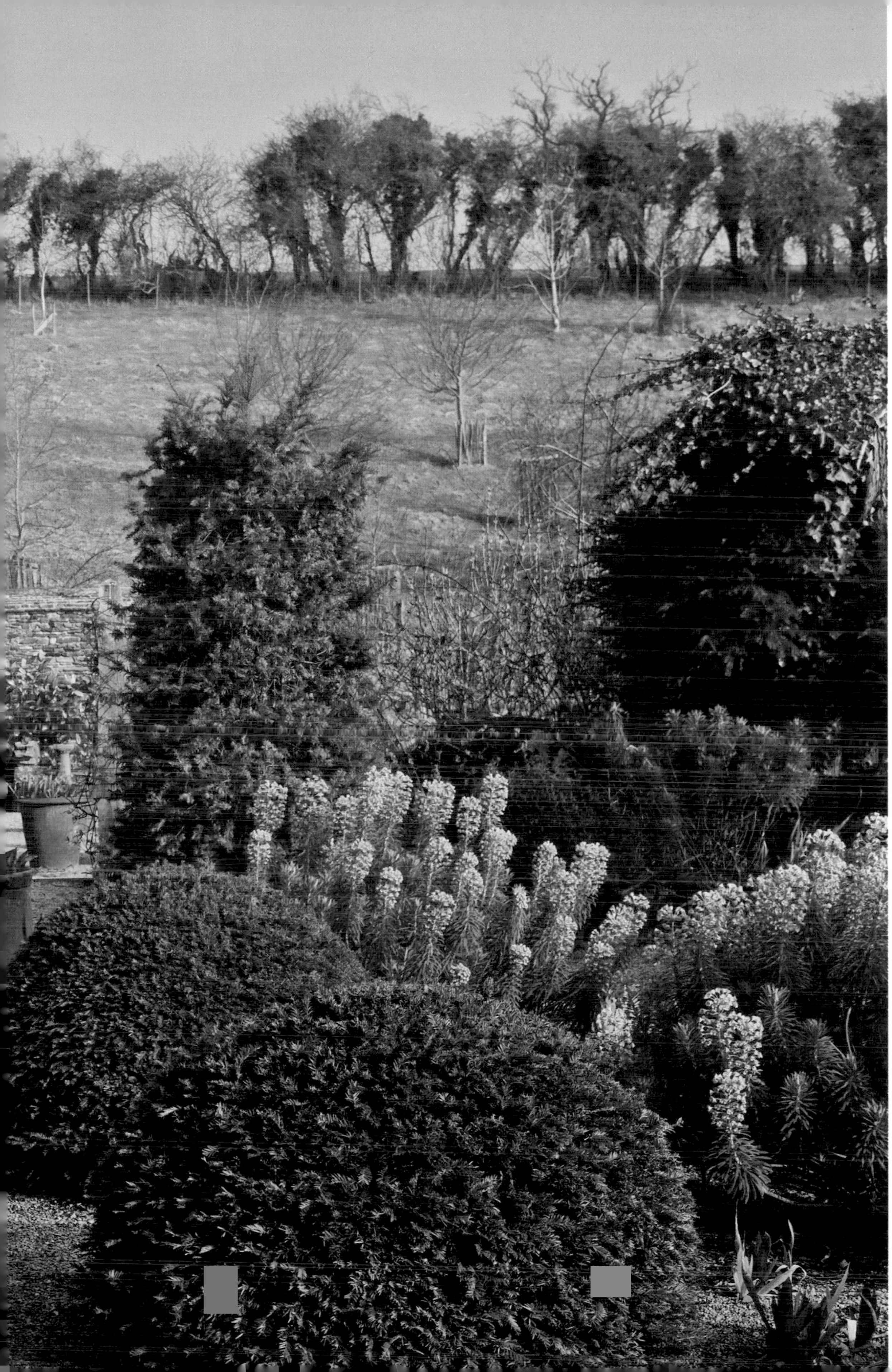

Outdoor Country

FEATHER DOWN FARM

GIVING A UNIQUE GLIMPSE INTO THE PAST AND FUTURE OF RURAL LIVING, FEATHER DOWN FARMS ENDORSE AN APPRECIATION OF THE SIMPLE THINGS IN LIFE, A PHILOSOPHY THAT LIES AT THE HEART OF CABBAGES & ROSES. THE BACKLASH AGAINST MASS PRODUCTION AND THE GREED OF THE 1980S AND 1990S HAS BROUGHT A NEWFOUND UNDERSTANDING THAT PRECIOUS RESOURCES SHOULD NOT BE WASTED OR TAKEN FOR GRANTED. THIS IS WHAT UNDERLINES THE MOVE TO CELEBRATE SIMPLICITY, BEAUTY, AND QUALITY OVER CONSUMERISM, FADS, AND FASHIONS.

Dotted around Britain and Holland, and soon to be established in America and France, Feather Down farms were the inspired idea of Dutch architect Luite Moraal. Not only do they provide a means of supplementing the income of hard-pressed farmers, but they also provide an enchanting

OPPOSITE, CLOCKWISE FROM TOP LEFT On a Feather Down farm vacation, a giant kettle provides hot water for washing and drinking, and butter from the farm shop is freshly churned on the premises. Each tent is positioned with a view of uninterrupted countryside, so the occupants are blissfully unaware of other tents pitched nearby. A printed linen tablecloth cheers up the picnic table laid for tea. Matching deckchairs offer additional seating to supplement the farm's large handmade chairs.

LEFT AND ABOVE RIGHT The farm shop is open all hours, selling produce that is either made on the farm or sourced locally. Cooking out in the open using the communal wood ovens made from rustic corrugated iron is a truly grounding experience.

real-life fantasy for anyone wishing to indulge in comfort with no impact on the environment.

Accommodation is in beautifully designed tents, carefully placed around a working farm, with beautiful views of farmland, woods, and rivers. They are run by the farmers and their families who live and work there, giving the added bonus of being exposed to local knowledge and of witnessing the custodianship exercised by the people who feed us by rearing animals and growing crops, as well as looking after our countryside.

Staying in comfort while living in the simplest way possible, and waking up in the middle of glorious rolling countryside, is a huge privilege in our overpopulated world, and this scheme offers a wonderful way to support such places. Staying at a Feather Down farm is made even better by the knowledge that you are contributing to the local community and culture—fishing, meandering through the local woodland, or joining in the tending of the farm.

WAKING UP TO COLLECT FRESHLY LAID EGGS FROM THE CHICKENS THAT WANDER ABOUT IN FRONT OF THE TENT IS A GROUNDING EXPERIENCE.

LEFT Simple creature comforts are provided and every tent is equipped with a hand-crank coffee grinder—beans are sold in the farm shop. Guests can enjoy freshly laid eggs in the china egg cups, which fit perfectly into the understated environment of the tent.

OPPOSITE Old fruit crates have been turned into a rustic version of built-in shelves; as well as providing storage, they double up as walls dividing the rooms. The storm lantern suspended from the ceiling, safely away from the bedclothes, reflects gentle light around the tent after the sun has gone down.

LEFT The tent is a good size, and even if the weather fails, it provides ample shelter and warmth from the central wood-burning stove. The cozy bed inside a wooden cupboard makes a perfect spot for an afternoon nap or for a sleepy child to nestle.

ABOVE A single tap provides cold water, which has to be heated up in the ample kettle on the wood-burning stove.

BELOW Nature in all its colorful glory is evident all around the tent, with grassy banks and fields of wild flowers.

LIVING AND SLEEPING IN A TENT—ALBEIT A LUXURIOUS ONE—IS A GREAT WAY TO RECONNECT WITH NATURE AND REDISCOVER LIFE'S SIMPLE PLEASURES.

Feather Down Farms are an entirely carbon neutral operation. The frames of the tents are made with wood from sustainable forests; heat is provided by wood-burning stoves, the fuel delivered from the woodpile in a wheelbarrow; light is from candles and oil lamps—there are no intrusions from modern life.

The tents are left erected until late fall when the weather becomes inclement, and although basic, they are beautifully designed and extremely comfortable. The sturdy wooden frames have walls of robust canvas, which house soft, inviting mattresses and warm duvets. The interiors are furnished identically and charmingly. Bedding can be provided, but taking your own allows you to add a personal touch. Bed linen, tablecloths, and towels in a mixture of colorful floral prints and cheerful stripes boost the comfort factor in an instant and create a homey country feel.

OPPOSITE The walls, when not comprised of old wooden crates, are made from locally sourced sustainable wood, as are the bunk beds. Each tent sleeps five to six people, and the layout is so expertly designed that the relatively small space can easily accommodate so many people and all their paraphernalia.

ABOVE LEFT The cupboard bed can be closed off by shutting the doors, so that sleeping children will not be disturbed by grownups dining in the main room.

ABOVE RIGHT Concealed underneath the cupboard bed is ample storage for luggage and spare bedding.

OPPOSITE AND ABOVE With its sturdy wood frame, the double bed in the main bedroom of the tent has a solidity rarely found on a campsite. The canvas walls give the room a romantic quality, enhanced by the dappled sunlight shining through the gauze window. The fresh summery feel is reinforced by the use of bright cerise bedding. A child's folding stool is used as a bedside table for a pile of the farm's vintage books and a vase of wild flowers. Experiencing the charms of rural life from a simpler time now far in the past makes a stay on a Feather Down farm truly memorable.

CENTRAL PARK PICNIC

PICNICS EVOLVED FROM A TRADITION STARTED BY THE BRITISH GENTRY IN MEDIEVAL TIMES FOR HOLDING ELABORATE OUTDOOR FEASTS AT THEIR HUNTING PARTIES. IT NOW DESCRIBES ALL KINDS OF OUTDOOR DINING, WHEN PEOPLE GATHER TOGETHER OUTSIDE TO ENJOY THE LANDSCAPE, FRESH AIR, GOOD WEATHER, AND FOOD, WHETHER IT'S A GRAND BANQUET, A RELAXED TEA PARTY, OR AN INFORMAL BARBECUE.

From a group of rice pickers stopping for lunch in the paddy fields of Asia, to the fishermen in Alaska feasting outdoors after a successful fishing trip, to busy office workers sharing a hasty lunch in a London park, picnics have become instilled in every culture across the globe. A sunny weekend in the summer invariably sees the greater part of the urban population flocking to the seaside, countryside, or a local park with hampers of food, disposable barbecues, and high spirits.

Central Park in New York City is a popular urban picnic spot for the residents of Manhattan. Among the bustle of wedding parties searching for the perfect spot for a photograph to capture their happy day, and the flurry of tourists and entertainers, it is the perfect place to entertain, relax, and eat wonderful food presented in a feast-like spread, with none of the restrictions a

THIS PAGE AND OPPOSITE A picnic in the park is a fine opportunity to take your kitschiest Tupperware and colorful picnic kit on a grand outing to a shady spot under a tree. Lay out all the food on a large washable cloth and provide plenty of pillows and cushions to lounge on. Cerise pillows and a striped linen cloth are the perfect complement to the cheerful red-and-white plates.

ABOVE AND OPPOSITE For an informal picnic lunch in Central Park, the country garden feel of the multicolored floral cloth with its old-fashioned rambling flowers provides a pleasing counterpoint to the backdrop of high-rise buildings. This is a scene created for pure escapism, in which it is easy to while away a lazy afternoon and forget the urban sprawl around you.

narrow table would present. The powerful backdrop of skyscrapers, offices, and grand residential buildings set against the serenity of the park serves as a constant reminder that this is an oasis in the heart of an urban jungle. Yet the high-powered offices and places of work are not quite able to penetrate the mood of fun and relaxation, created in such a simple way by the use of a pretty cloth and a pile of comfy pillows.

Picnics are all about setting the scene—whether it's fun and kitsch, extravagant and opulent, or nostalgic and romantic. I am a true believer in taking the indoor comforts we are all accustomed to, such as linen tablecloths, pillows, and cushions, outside. Linen is a strikingly hardy material that

becomes more beautiful every time it is washed, so a few grass stains and a little dampness seem irrelevant if it means you can doze off comfortably after a long al fresco feast. Picnic plates and glasses can be as grand or as informal as you like—just make sure they are light to carry and easy to clean.

PICNICKING IS A CHANCE TO ADAPT A PIECE OF COMMON GROUND, TO TEMPORARILY CREATE A SPACE OF YOUR OWN WITH EASILY TRANSPORTABLE KIT THAT YOU CAN PACK UP AT THE END OF AN ENJOYABLE DAY.

OPPOSITE The steep slopes of the vegetable garden are enclosed by an iron fence to keep deer away from the homegrown produce. A border of fragrant lavender bushes separates the working parts of the garden—the orchard and vegetable garden—from the pool area.

RIGHT White-painted chairs are kept outside all year round and are frequently used for an evening drink, weather permitting. Cushions and pillows are often taken from around the house to make a very comfortable outdoor terrace to relax on and take in the views, while inconspicuously decorating one of our favorite spots.

BELOW Freestanding wire obelisks are wonderful climbing frames, letting the sweet peas peek above anything else growing around them in the garden.

OUTSIDE AT BROOK COTTAGE

BROOK COTTAGE STANDS AT THE BOTTOM OF A SPECTACULAR VALLEY, WITH GREEN HILLS RISING UP ON EITHER SIDE AND A BROOK RUNNING ALONG THE BOUNDARY AT THE BOTTOM OF THE GARDEN. THE SHEER STEEPNESS OF THE GROUND POSED SOME PROBLEMS WHEN IT CAME TO DESIGNING THE GARDEN, BUT WE HAVE WORKED AROUND THEM AND HAVE COME UP WITH VERY CREATIVE SOLUTIONS AS A RESULT.

The unusual and dramatic pool is one such solution. The limestone surround sits level with the base of the tree canopies at the bottom of the garden, giving a swimmer the impression of being suspended in midair, elevated above the valley. Both the pool and house are heated by a wood-burning stove, the wood supplied from trees felled on our land and in the surrounding sustainably managed woodland—key to reducing our carbon footprint.

The pool, while being hidden from much of the garden, has a perfect vantage point over the fields opposite and the brook below, the surrounding pots and plants helping it to merge in with the rest of the landscape. Warmed by the early morning sun, it is the perfect place to start the day.

ABOVE The hidden tree house nestles into the hill and small area of woodland near the edge of the garden border. The slope drops away sharply, leaving it suspended up in the trees. Many old trinkets are kept inside an old gym locker, ready to be used for a day of painting or creativity.

Reaching up the hill are beds of fragrant lavender bordering the vegetable garden, which is surrounded by a fence to keep out the deer. Not only does the working garden provide fresh produce for the family all year round, I have also managed to squeeze in some ornamental plants—mini cabbages, roses, and sweet peas; even some poppies have found their own little patch. The

ABOVE The extended collection of white china jugs and pitchers has spilled from the kitchen onto the shelves in the tree house, playing the part of a piece of artwork. The guest room has a perfect area in which to sit and read on a quiet afternoon in this tranquil airy space in the trees.

garden is ordered, but there is still room for nature to make a few decisions, making it easier to maintain and nurturing a slightly wilder kind of beauty.

The tree house suspended in the trees over the brook was built for the children when they were seven and nine years old, and proved to be a wonderful summertime playhouse. It has since been extended to create

FRESH SPRINGS TRICKLE DOWN FROM THE HILLS, GIVING THE GARDEN A FEELING OF VIBRANCY AND LIFE, WITH THE REFRESHING NOISE OF THE WATER SOURCES BUBBLING ALONG THEIR VARIOUS CHANNELS.

a workspace and studio, and has gradually developed into an unusual guest room (for the not-so-fainthearted). The three trees that spike through the floor and rise through the ceiling do allow a few small visitors in, but it is watertight and sufficiently warm in the winter with the use of a small wood-burning stove.

Each season we completely re-dress the tree house. It has proven to be something of a chameleon over the years—cozy and inviting with deep red rugs and blankets, or light, white, and refreshing, as it is here. The informality of the simple wood structure makes it an extra joy to play with, as this liberates you from the worry of not doing something as properly as you might with a plaster wall or a limestone floor.

The large tent has been a part of our family for more than a decade. Even though the canvas is beginning to look a little tired, each year we count

down the days until we can pull out the seagrass matting and move some comfortable furniture into our "new outside sitting room." We often get overexcited far too soon and end up dining swathed in layers of coats and scarves, eating a cold supper or lunch in sub-zero spring temperatures—but it still holds its charm. A favorite occupation is to sit under the canopy during a tremendous thunderstorm and enjoy the drama of fat raindrops bouncing off the canvas with the fresh smell of damp earth filtering inside.

A tent such as this will always be the most effective entertaining tool for a family living in a small house, removing all of the constraints of limited indoor space and a restricted guest list. It is a truly magical place at nighttime, with fairy lights and candles twinkling in the breeze against the backdrop of the old apple tree and flowerbeds in the garden beyond.

OPPOSITE Trestle tables are used all around the tent and can be rearranged next to each other to create a huge dining table for entertaining crowds of people. Flowers picked from the surrounding beds and borders draw the green backdrop of the garden inside the tent. The antique linen tablecloths are hardy enough to withstand the outdoor elements.

LEFT AND ABOVE This reupholstered French-style formal sofa contrasts sharply with the nature surrounding it. The gentle blue tones of the Cabbages & Roses prints on the linen cushions complement the faded hues around the tent, from the display of cream candles used for atmospheric lighting in the evenings, to the metal lanterns and frosted-glass candlesticks accumulated over the years.

The tent transforms into a completely different room in the evening. Waterproof fairy lights and storm lanterns enable the candle flames to withstand any breeze filtering through the open room, while the draped linen across the roof brings a rather exotic Eastern influence to the scene.

FABRIC DIRECTORY

These swatches represent our current range of Cabbages & Roses' fabrics. Do check our website (www.cabbagesandroses.com) for any new designs or colorways and for ordering details.

BELLEVUE

Multi stripe	Blue 3-inch stripe	Raspberry 3-inch stripe
India Rose	Tulips and Roses	Natural Hatley, blue
		Natural Hatley, raspberry
French Toile, raspberry	French Toile, aqua	Natural Meggernie, blue
		Natural Meggernie, raspberry

AGNES

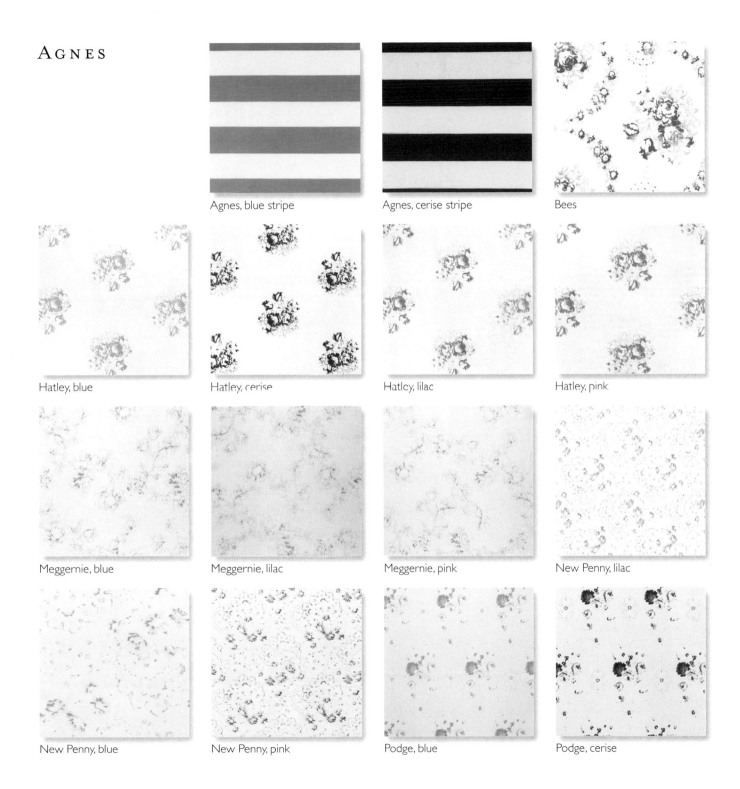

Agnes, blue stripe

Agnes, cerise stripe

Bees

Hatley, blue

Hatley, cerise

Hatley, lilac

Hatley, pink

Meggernie, blue

Meggernie, lilac

Meggernie, pink

New Penny, lilac

New Penny, blue

New Penny, pink

Podge, blue

Podge, cerise

LANGTON

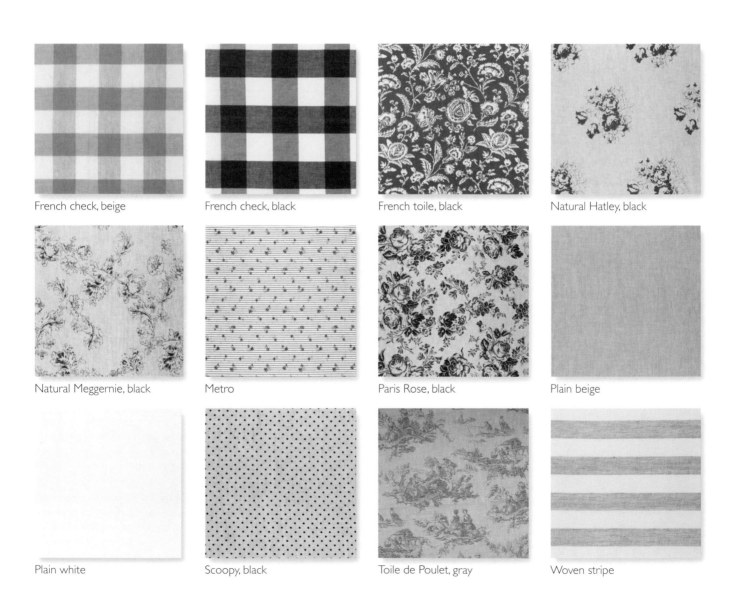

French check, beige

French check, black

French toile, black

Natural Hatley, black

Natural Meggernie, black

Metro

Paris Rose, black

Plain beige

Plain white

Scoopy, black

Toile de Poulet, gray

Woven stripe

REGENTS

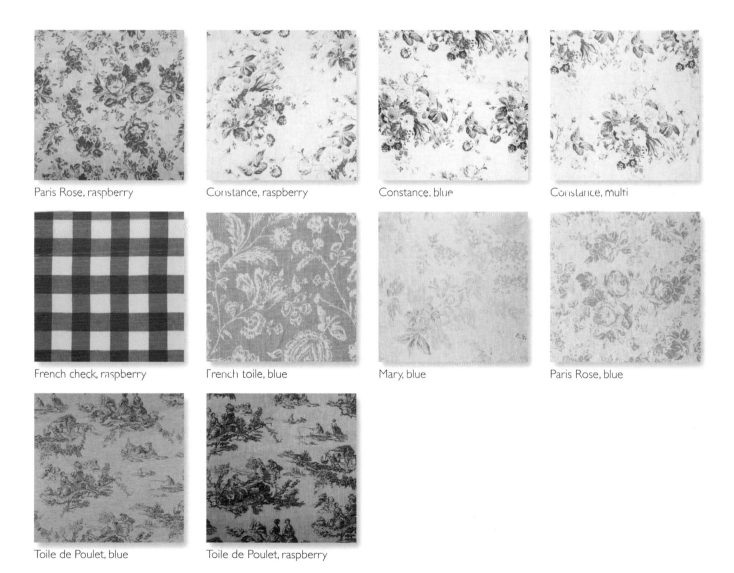

Paris Rose, raspberry

Constance, raspberry

Constance, blue

Constance, multi

French check, raspberry

French toile, blue

Mary, blue

Paris Rose, blue

Toile de Poulet, blue

Toile de Poulet, raspberry

INDEX

AUTHOR'S ACKNOWLEDGMENTS

It has been a thrilling journey making this book, especially for Amy Gibbons who, more than once, has been thrown in at the deep end and, with her usual calm and sensibilities, stepped into the breach at a moment's notice; Edina van der Wyck who fulfilled the roles of driver, map reader, entertainer, and photographer extraordinaire; and Kate Strutt, who with two weeks' notice, wrote the beautiful words. I joined in—at the end! The entire idea was the brainchild of my dear friend Françoise O'Neill who, as creator of this project, has also encouraged us along the way, alongside editing magazines, filming television programs, and entertaining a million people on her blog.

Thank you to all at CICO Books involved in creating this, our fifth book, especially Cindy Richards, Gillian Haslam, Sally Powell, and Paul Tilby.

Our thanks also to the kind home owners who allowed the Cabbages & Roses team into their lives with grace and hospitality, especially my dear friends Julian and Isabelle Bannerman of Hanham Court, Bristol whose home and garden are now open to the public; Lucy and Patrick Woodroffe for allowing us to photograph their boat and home; and the ever-resourceful Sarah Callander-Beckett and her American address book.

Thank you to all at Cabbages & Roses, especially Amy Gibbons, Linda Cardona, Rian Howells, Nichola Hunt, Monika Cakova, Sabine Kokles, and Kate Strutt.

To the Strutt family, as always.

And last but not least, to my mother Mary Amoroso-Centeno, Joanna Hayes, and Dr Shakir for averting what might have been a crisis!

OUR THANKS ALSO TO:

Designer and author, Tricia Foley
Tricia Foley Design, New York City, New York
tricia@triciafoley.com
www.triciafoley.com

Ellen O'Neill
eoneill@ellenoneillsupply.com

Diane M Good
Good & White, 635 West Falmouth Highway,
West Falmouth, MA 02574
TGood1@adelphia.net
www.goodandwhite.com

Julian and Isabel Bannerman Design
Hanham Court Gardens, Ferry Road, Hanham Abbots,
Bristol, South Gloucestershire BS15 3NT
info@hanhamcourt.co.uk
www.hanhamcourt.co.uk

Andrew Bernstein and Jenny Chase
andrew@andrewbernsteininc.com
www.andrewbernsteininc.com

jenny@jennychaseinc.com
www.jennychaseinc.com

Feather Down Farm
Manor Farm, West Worldham, near Alton, Hampshire
info@featherdown.co.uk
www.featherdownfarm.co.uk

Will Tricket Boats
williamtrickett@hotmail.co.uk
www.trickettboats.com

Michael Steinberg and Suzanna Steinburg
Pointed Leaf Press
www.pointedleafpress.com

Michael Steinberg Fine Art
www.michaelsteinbergfineart.com

CABBAGES & ROSES

For information on Cabbages and Roses shops and stockists, and for mail order, please visit our website:
www.cabbagesandroses.com
info@cabbagesandroses.com

For US trade customers, Cabbages & Roses' fabrics are also stocked through:
J. Lambeth & Company, Washington Design Center
www.jlambeth.com

4144